Astronaut

Lucy M. George

AndoTwin

Jenny, Chen and Kim are astronauts. They are going into space!

They have been training for a long time, and now it's the big day.

A long time ago,
astronauts landed
on the moon.

LIKE?

NOT LIKE?

...as
...lars to
...face.
...be to
go there one day.

The space station is a long way away.
It's time to board the space shuttle!

Mission Control count down...

5..4..3..2...1...Blast Off!

Jenny and the astronauts soar up...up...up and away from Earth.

They whizz through
the atmosphere.

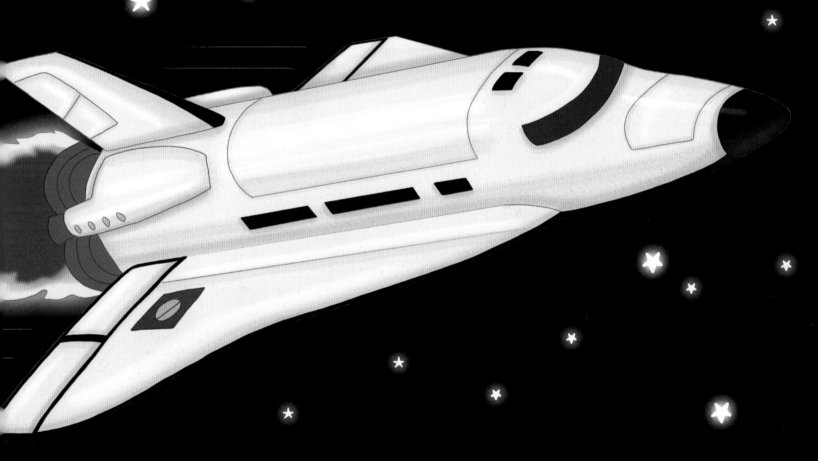

The space shuttle releases its rockets
and before they know it they're
in deep, dark, incredible space!

Finally, they reach
the space station.

The crew and Robo-bot are
waiting to welcome them.

"Hello!" Jenny says.

"Beep boop!" greets Robo-bot.

Robo-bot loves to help clean the space station.
He tickles Jenny with his feather duster!

Jenny speaks to Mission Control.
It's time for a spacewalk!

Jenny and Chen are going
to observe small rocky
objects called asteroids.

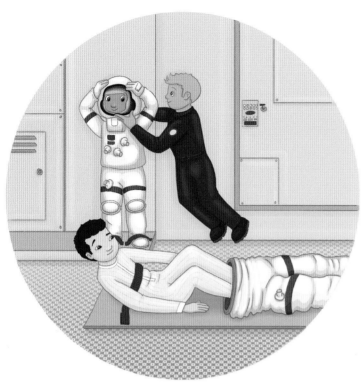

Jenny and Chen put on their spacesuits and helmets.

They go to the hatch and exit the airlock.

"Good luck!" shout the crew.

Jenny and Chen are floating in space!

"WOW!"
Jenny cries.

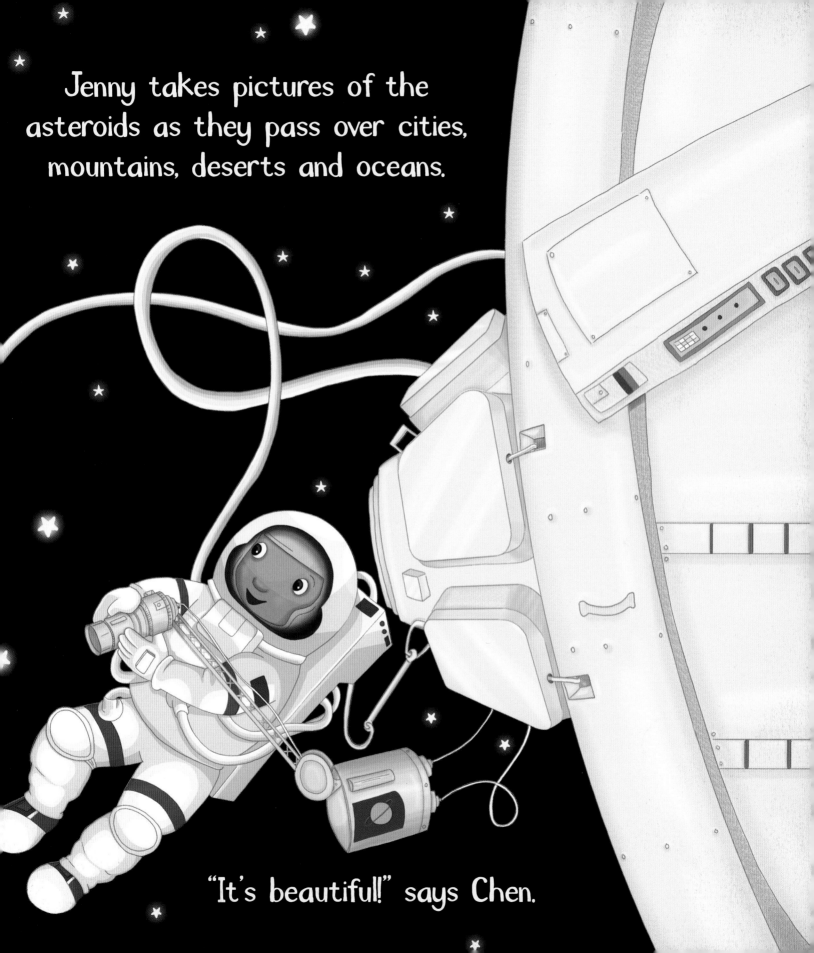

Jenny takes pictures of the asteroids as they pass over cities, mountains, deserts and oceans.

"It's beautiful!" says Chen.

When they've finished, they go to the hatch.
"It's stuck," says Chen.

Jenny and Chen work away and
heave the hatch open! Phew!

Inside the space station,
everything is out of place!

"Got you!" Jenny cries, quickly fixing Robo-bot
before he can cause any more trouble.

What a day!
It's time to relax
and have dinner.

When they've finished,
Robo-bot cleans up.
The crew watch
nervously but Robo-bot
puts everything
away carefully.

Before bed, Jenny calls her family on Earth below and tells them all about her busy day,

Then she brushes her teeth. It can be tricky in space!

Jenny decides to switch Robo-bot off for the night... just in case!

Jenny waves to her beautiful home planet far below.

"Goodnight, World," she says.

What else does Jenny do?

Cleans and repairs equipment.

Conducts scientific experiments.

Records data.

Keeps fit and healthy.

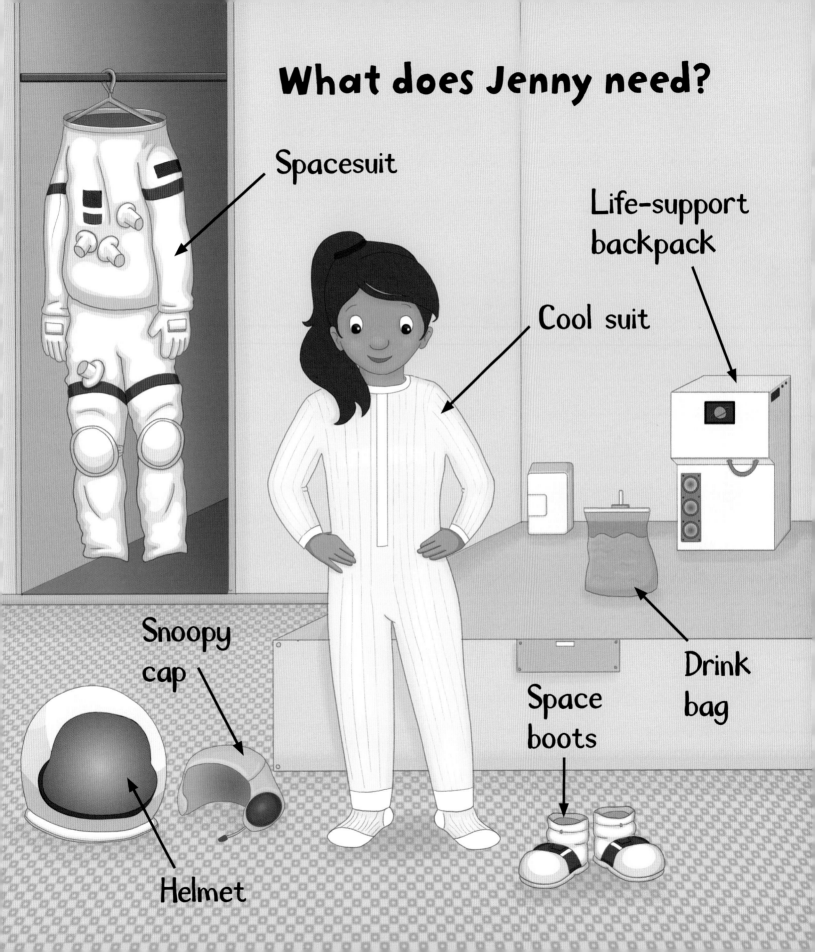

Other busy people

Here are some of the other busy people astronauts work with.

Flight controllers look after space shuttles coming in and out of space. They help run the space station, speaking to astronauts from the ground every day.

Flight directors are in charge of the team of flight controllers. They look after the smooth running of the space program and plan future trips to space.

Engineers design, test and make almost everything for space exploration, from the shuttles to spacesuits and food warmers to toilets!

Scientists design experiments to be conducted in space and guide astronauts over the phone as they do the experiments. They collect and analyse data sent back from space.

$$\Phi_D = L_{eff}(V_x) V_x B_{YZ} \sin^{9/2} \tfrac{1}{2}\theta,$$
$$L_{eff}(V_x) = 3.8 R_E \left(\frac{V_x}{4 \times 10^5 ms^{-1}} \right)^{1/3}$$

Next steps

- Did you know there was a space station orbiting Earth? Can you think of some reasons why humans are interested in exploring space?

- What did Jenny and Chen do while they were outside the space station? Research where the asteroid belt is in the solar system. Draw the solar system with the asteroid belt.

- Jenny and Chen wore special spacesuits on their spacewalk. Why do you think they wore them? How do you think they might have felt about going into space?

- There's almost no gravity in space, which means everything feels light and floaty. What do you think would be difficult in space and why? What do you think would be easier in space than on Earth?

- The astronauts were nervous when Robo-bot was cleaning up dinner – why was that? What other jobs could robots do in space? Why would they be better suited than humans for these jobs?

Publisher: Maxime Boucknooghe
Editorial Director: Victoria Garrard
Art Director: Miranda Snow
Editor: Sophie Hallam
Designer: Victoria Kimonidou

Copyright © QED Publishing 2016

First published in the UK in 2016 by
QED Publishing
Part of The Quarto Group
The Old Brewery
6 Blundell Street
London, N7 9BH

www.qed-publishing.co.uk

A catalogue record for this book is available from the British Library.

ISBN 978 1 78493 150 6

Printed in China

For Granny Wilson

– AndoTwin

For Laura

– Lucy M. George